INTIMACY WITH THE WIND

poems by

Carla Schwartz

Finishing Line Press
Georgetown, Kentucky

SOW THE WIND

INTIMACY WITH THE WIND

Copyright © 2017 by Carla Schwartz
ISBN 978-1-63534-309-0 First Edition
All rights reserved under International and Pan-American Copyright Conventions.
No part of this book may be reproduced in any manner whatsoever without written permission from the publisher, except in the case of brief quotations embodied in critical articles and reviews.

Publisher: Leah Maines

Editor: Christen Kincaid

Cover Art: "Wake with the Sun at Valcour Island" original photo
       by Carla Schwartz

Author Photo: Claude von Roesgen

Cover Design: Elizabeth Maines McCleavy

Printed in the USA on acid-free paper.
Order online: www.finishinglinepress.com
       also available on amazon.com

Author inquiries and mail orders:
Finishing Line Press
P. O. Box 1626
Georgetown, Kentucky 40324
U. S. A.

Table of Contents

I
Photoshopping the Body 1
Moving Slips 2
At Breakfast 4
Trying to Leave Mallets Bay 6
Comment se Faire 8
My Father's Hiking Boots 10
Lost Hour 11
To the Toilet 12
Dry Period 14
2014 16
When I Dig a Hole 18
Dawn 19
City Bay to Butler Island in the Solar-powered Boat 20
To Seize the Ice 21
The Day His Mother Died 22
Aubade for Champlain 24

II
Celestial Events 27
The Escape 28
Volunteering with the Immigrant Mothers 29
Black Trumpets 30
Becoming Calm 31
Left Ear 32
Imaginary Ice 33
Nick Flynn Reads *My Feelings* 34
Holiday 36
Gum Surgery 37
Roadside Apples, Vermont 38
Check Engine Light 39
Among the Pine Chips 40
Notes from the Green Room 41
Houseboat Song 42
The Mistake of Cutting Down 43
Our Dance 44

III

Intimacy with the Wind 47
Asparagus 48
Learning to Ride 50
To a Spur Trail 52
Gummi 53
Invasive Species 54
Cormorant Convention 56
Snapshots 57
September, Champlain 58
Shadows through the Window 60
Hot and Cold 61
Everywhere, the Light 62
Oh, Thistle 63
Late for Dinner 64
Bedrooms 65
Dream 68

IV

Invasive Species on the Trail 73
Valcour 74
My Orchard 76
Sunshine State 77
Before We Know Darkness 78
A Passion Fruit 79
To Abuse 80
Something from Nothing 81
In My Yard 82
On the Ocean 84
Solar House Living 85
The Sad Ballad of the Garlic Mustard 86
Raspberry Season 87
My Netherland 88
Reasons, November 90
Crisis, 1962 92
Rings 93
Acknowledgements

To Claude, for every waking moment

I

Photoshopping the Body

Surely my mother would have known what to do.
Would have understood *Masking*,
Healing. Once, she used Illustrator to make a rainbow
Medusa of my sister's hair. That was back in the 90s,
when nothing was obvious. She was just that kind of woman,
to dive into a computer program & wrangle
with it, until she got what she wanted.

For this image of me in my bikini,
she would have been a *Magic Wand*
wizard, smoothing out the wrinkles & shadows,
removing the thickness around the thighs,
that same belly, those same thick thighs she bore,
with the click + drag of a mouse, wouldn't she?

To look in the mirror, & see my mother's rounded body,
the sunburst of skin from the naval, the rays, the folds,
the darker, vertical depression that leads netherward,
what I was once embarrassed of for her, saddens me.

My mother never wore a bikini,
but would have relished summers on this lake,
to swim every morning, after waking just a few steps from shore.

My mother, if only she were here, would sit with me
overlooking the lake, wearing shorts & oversized T,
an iPad in hand, never mind her belly,
& swipe, tap, hold.

Moving Slips

They swished
against her dress or skirt
as she moved,
one leg following the next,
like the eyes
behind her
as she walked.

When she died,
we picked up
the folded slips,
still scented,
a faint of lavender,
the pinks, the beiges,
the fulls and halves,
and boxed them
for Goodwill.

Today I moved slips.
I worried over the moves
I would make
for a day and night,
one handle of future
I thought I could control.

First, I would reverse
straight and clear,
leave the one slip behind,
before I would turn
and drive
toward the next.

But wind,
no matter how much
I plan,
has the upper hand.
When she blows
hard enough to knock,
all I can do
is react.

At Breakfast

Out at the glass table, under the cloudless sky, on the deck, by the lake,
my cousin David tells me our neurologist Grandpa examined a famous serial killer.

Son of Sam, he thought. *No,* I say, Grandpa was already dead, then.
I googled it. Maybe, Howard Unruh.

Unruh, a war veteran, had planned for two years.
A Lugar, a knife, *paranoia*—back then, it wasn't called post-traumatic stress.

My father said the killer had a newspaper name. I googled again.
Maybe, the *Lonely Hearts Killer,* Ramond Fernandez.

Finally, Aunt Marge thought she knew—*Boston Strangler*—DeSalvo,
thirteen women, assaulted and strangled. *I'm sorry*, DeSalvo admitted.

Our grandfather died before David was born. I was only six.
I had known only that he was a doctor for Holocaust refugees.

It turns out he was also the chief psychiatrist in a prison hospital
for New York's criminally insane.

I remember a big, round man in a wool jacket and bow tie, even in summer.
Always a cigar in his mouth, and his incessant pleas for a kiss, which scared me.

Now, I see in his photo, my mother's *Daddy*,
with her same sweet, gentle smile.

I don't think Unruh had a newspaper name.
Marge concedes she must be mistaken about the Strangler. I'm betting on Fernandez.

As we finish our eggs, David adds that my mother burned
some of my grandfather's scholarly work after his death.

Once more, I google the faulty family database
about this news.

My father says, *She never burned them.*
Marge, *She feared the Germans would come after them.*

Trying to Leave Mallets Bay

This morning the waves are ducks waddling on the surface,
not scary, as we start off from the land that makes up the shore,
a wall, but not a solid one, a lace curtain buffer,
so not all the wind comes through here,
not the off-shore winds.

Stocked for a few days' travel,
we motor out at our usual *walking* pace.
Our boat, like a floating elephant—
a small cape house on pontoons,
solar-powered, electric motor,
A tortoise, not a hare,
and as the wind picks up from the south and west,
we head north on these waves
that have graduated from ducks to dolphins,
and ride the seesaw.

These waves mean business,
like the bureaucrats at the registry downtown—
no beating them.

We could stop right now, turn back,
but we've been trapped here for days,
and want to get out into the big lake,
so we hope for calm in this, the bad-ass lower bay,
protected from the fetch of the outer bay, and motor on,
wishing away the pummeling the wind has in store for us.

The further we go, the bigger the waves.
In the outer bay, whales of them
pound the boat from the side,
breaching half the deck,
and sound as loud as a washing machine
gone berserk.

You stand like Liberty
and measure the wind,
as if that will change our minds,
keep us from turning back.

These winds, fierce,
and we have not even met
the wide open lake.

Comment se Faire

The theatre was near the Grand Place,
convenient for *moules et frites*
and a short walk to the train, afterward.

The cinema, ornate, but worn,
with molded balconies, velvet curtains
and red carpet.

Ushers and restroom attendants expected tips.
My first day in Brussels,
I held my bags tight.

I took my place in the middle of the middle,
an empty row, where I could spread my bags
on the seat to my right.

Comment Faire l'Amour avec un Nègre sans se Fatiguer,
a Canadian film, sparsely attended—
the unemployed, the retired, and me.

I focused on the language, French,
and the Montreal neighborhoods I knew—
Carré St. Louis, Rue St. Denis,

when, of all open seats,
a man selected the chair, two seats to my right.
I bristled and swung my belongings to my left.

Another man moved in then,
on that side, and I was sandwiched,
my bags between my legs,

while Man Number 1 moved to the seat next to mine,
and Number 2 closed in on my left.
I stayed put, rather than getting up to move.

When my row mates began to pant and rub,
I tensed my grip on my camera, my purse,
my neck craned like a stargazer.

The men left before intermission,
but I stayed fixed, until the end,
when I walked away from a small death.

My Father's Hiking Boots

On Saturdays, my father wakes to the old G.E. alarm
that buzzes him from the open-jawed stupor he prefers,
and bends around to push himself up from bed.

Now, his cranky knees slow him,
so he wakes earlier to turn on the radio,
swirls rinse between his cheeks,

throws a couple of sweet potatoes in the *nuker*,
to pack for lunch, fills a water bottle, fills a bowl with cereal,
fills his time until he's ready for the *crapper*.

He picks up his boots, the current ones, at the door—
not the several pairs of never worn, next-in-lines,
brands he trusts—Vasque, Keene, Teva,

bought on sale over the years, waiting patiently in his closet.

How many of these pairs will remain unused when he's gone?

He grabs his keys and poles
and clicks the garage door open through the window.
Soon, he'll blame the stones he trips on.

Lost Hour

Last week
I lost the poem I wrote
about the extra hour
I wish I had,
it was a great poem,
I peppered the lines
with poignant commentary
and smart observations
about how I would fill the hour.

Of course, I have forgotten most of these,
but it was a powerful poem—
the hour, perched
above the hour we traded
for spring last week,
the hyacinths poking up,
the peach buds coaxed open
by a warm spell,
then nipped by cold and snow—
that wasn't even the best part,
I cycled a wooded trail,
divulged where that lost hour really goes
while contemplating a lion's mane of chives,
bright green, emerging from the dark soil,
but not that mundane,
much better,
and I'm still searching for it—
the poem,
the extra hour,
the lost one.

To the Toilet

Toilet, new toilet,
composting toilet,
usurper of a behemoth,
the fishing crate of the original
Clivus Multrum, the big, boxy,
homeless throne that never made it into the tiny house,
where every square inch
of its one hundred twenty eight square feet counts.

You, ordinary, cream-colored toilety looking thing,
huddled in your corner, like a Persian cat,
your size, a small trash can,
your volume, extruded from the footprint of the seat
lidded and black-handled, a crank,
like on an old-fashioned ice-cream maker or a butter churn,
efficient concealer of sheet rock bucket and gallon jug,
and aptly named, C-Head,
so petite, so perfect,
Claude runs to tell me each time he uses you,
insisting I will love you too,
but that I must practice, getting right with you,
while to myself, I think
how difficult can you be? and avoid you.

What worse failure than to fail at toilet,
and what would that mean?

To sit, and sit,
and sit, and wait,
for the filling of the blank page,
while my mind wanders,
and the page remains pristine
with overconscious embarrassment,
and I think about a room,
about constructing a room of my own
out of the whole cloth of the blank, white sheet
I tie with bands and loops,
the tie-dyed pink medusa,
I pull from the washing machine,
cut and sew as curtain, as wall,
a room we might share
a rose haven for the waste.

Dry Period

The swim shirt hangs on the line
sun-warmed,
still moist.

My skin, dry.
My father applies
Vaseline.

The lake so low,
the dock doesn't reach
water's edge.

The fishing birds
of early summer—herons, eagles,
gone.

The fish
who nibbled algae on the rocks,
gone.

The rocks,
once blips at water's height,
now prominent, white with guano.

The cormorants,
with tapered snake beaks,
watch for minnows.

They dry their wings,
pose for photos, unfazed,
study the photographers.

The pine trees,
stressed by drought,
the dead needles, like tears fall.

The peonies, the lawns,
dried, brown,
might not return.

A cairn artist
builds a stone family
at the pond's edge—

Auntie, lain down to rest,
children, parents,
cousins.

The stones emerge
mostly dry
above the lapping water.

2014

Late summer morning, 2014. The sun, still low enough
to cast shadows of the towels hanging on the deck lines.

A woman in a red floral print bikini, folded
onto a purple yoga mat on deck,

the mat, too, folded under her head.
The photographer's shadow, longer than the others,

brushes her feet. Behind her sunglasses, you cannot see
her eyes sparkle at the photographer, but her smile, evidence.

2014, Hillary, just ready to declare candidacy,
Isis, their caliphate, the search for Malaysian Airlines 370.

The woman in this photograph,
one hand, over her head, like a fainting debutante,

the other flat on her belly, target
of the camera.

So as not to declare the size of her hips,
she forms an "s" with them along the plank lines.

She thinks about the meal she will cook that evening,
about the photographer, the man she lives with, only in summer.

He thinks, she can't fall and hurt herself just lying there,
can't break anything, and relaxes. 2014, his mother,

not seen in this photograph, grabbed the hands
of her embracing arms and shook them vigorously.

She wipes her forehead and sucks in her gut. There is
blind hope. They feel it in the breeze.

They don't know that next year at this time,
he will lose his mother, and on that night

as they sleep, the boat will rock and rock
and shake them awake.

Time has passed, but stupid grudges
are not the only truth about how we proceed.

The mother dies before the possibility of reconciliation,
and when the dinner hour arrives,

this couple, they hold each other,
they touch often, they dance under the stars.

When I Dig a Hole

When I dig this hole, and dig up
this sweet garlic mustard, I unearth
my neighbor's heart. How can that be?

After years of not more than a shared *Hello*,
I unearth her dig: *Unsightly.* Her thrust: *Mow it down.*
Her complaint, calling the town about my wildflowers
gone to seed. She once whined
my trees were going to fall on her house,
and welcomed my taking them down.
Now, over the undergrowth, she adds, *I love trees.*
I would never harm a tree.

What if someone had told me years ago:
If you would just marry, live conventionally,
let your husband care for your lawn
like all the other men in the neighborhood,
you would not have to strain your back
hacking away at your land—what
would I have said? What could I have answered,
every time someone did—*This is who I am,
this, my shovel?*

Dawn

After the pink
    comes blue.
The clouds reflect
    not all we see
is unimpeded sky.

City Bay to Butler Island in the Solar-powered Boat

I.
The sun, not fully risen
on the gray horizon.

The clouds, changeable,
white, lavender, silver.

The sky, bluing,
threatens to stay dark.

A docking rope,
collapsed in a corner.

The unstill waters, the shadows of wetness,
waves that lap the deck.

A wind from behind,
our friend, as we travel by sun.

II.
The wind overtakes the anchor,
and sets the boat adrift.

No matter. Our boat
has already made new friends.

We tie to their mooring,
we sleep without worry.

To Seize the Ice

Watch for signs the ice is solid—pay attention when a hard freeze follows a few
 cold days.
When driving around, make sure your skates are in the car, and a chair.
Let the subzero temperatures invite your inertia for coffee—overcome inertia
 while it's taking a piss.

When you miss that best but coldest skating day, don't pound yourself over that.
Set out the next day for a big shallow pond, a sure bet at 20 degrees, even with fresh
 snow.
Park off-road, careful your wheels won't get stuck on ice or in snow. Watch from
 your car,

a fisherman drags his sled and auger onto the ice. Don't wait any longer.
Grab your skates and chair. Leave the chair where you lace up and push off.
Be a sprite—get yourself stuck on the ice.

Stroke through the light layer of snow gracefully. Watch for holes and debris.
Skip over the rifts. Skate over your fears. Send them to the far reaches of the pond
where the reeds poke through the layers of ice and air—you won't go there.

Let your momentum take you down when your blades stop short in the snow. Don't
be startled when you fall. Don't be embarrassed that the ice fishermen see you.
When you realize you have wrenched your arm, months of therapy to come, why
 stop?

The sun, the ice, your skates. Float over thick sheets of crystal blackness.
Soar to the pong-pong, the shifting layers of ice against water.
Take care for the bumps you don't see and slide over the ones you do.

Skate until the shadows thicken.
Your blue chair waits alone at the shore, your beacon.
Fall softly into its embrace.

The Day His Mother Died

I bet you think it was a day like any other,
a happy couple, motoring out for a sunset cruise.
Not so much. It was a stunning day,
the winds, calm. No clouds.
By afternoon, the marina, a trailer park for boats—
the party boats, the dogs, the smokers, the crammed slips—
had worn on them,
and they headed north to anchor near a beach,
away from the city.

You think they canceled their dinner plan,
took care—where to set anchor,
the depth, the distance from shore,
from other boats—you'd guess?
Not so much. After the wait for the anchor to settle,
the swim around the boat to check it,
there was the solemn lie down,
spooned in the twin bed,
hands intertwined,
the wait for a nap.

Later, he would ferry their guest by kayak.
Do you think he mentioned anything en route?
Probably not. She would stay on the boat,
to prepare the salad, the one-pot lentils and rice,
started an hour earlier, red lentils that cook fast,
with mushrooms, onions, and spices.

Do you think their guest noticed,
whenever they passed close enough,
their ready affection,
the hands that closed the gap between them?
After the dinner, cherry pie on the deck,
a brilliant sunset reflected in the window,
and no one cracked. The evening was perfect,
don't you think?

Did she look whole, having slept so little?
What if I say he'd taken a hotel room, the night before,
and she'd been ready to walk out that morning,
except for that matter of the sunshine on a fresh day,
and her bad-girl harbor swim,
then, the run-in with the coastguard that made them both laugh,
until he read a mangled transcription of his voicemail
and looked up to her with the news in his eyes,
and their rift of the day before, a mere fault in a rock,
not insurmountable, if they paid attention.

Aubade for Champlain

You could have been placid this morning,
like yesterday, smooth, soft,
with tiny frills gathered,
as the wind whispered across
your great expanse.

You could have slept in,
muffled snores erupting
from the north,
or conjectured the next solution
to global warming,

or just bathed as you stirred
cyanobacterial algae
into intricate patterns
of paisley swirls,
arced stripes.

But the sun peeks
from behind moist clouds,
wisps of lather,
tongue,
hot pink,

and on a day that has not yet decided what to do with itself,
egged by the wind,
you roar your steady roar,
throw yourself, and throw again,
let spring a force worthy of the heat to come,

something I can fight against
with all my might,
stroke, after stroke.
As I swim, wash over me,
wave,
wave.

II

Celestial Events

The spring equinox coincides
with a solar eclipse
and the phone rings,
your mother.

The sun splits the day in half
and the moon lines up to pass
between the earth and sun.

Someone, somewhere, some camera
will watch, some trick of mirrors,
and post it to the internet.

When your mother calls,
just before you board,
she starts in with the weather,
and you tell her,
flying,
you say, *skiing*,
she says, *Easter*,
next weekend,
she says, *Sister*,
she says, *Please*,
and you want to please,
so you don't quite say *No*
before you board,
before you end the call.

So she calls back,
the plane, still on the tarmac,
says, *Wait, you must understand,*
and you already know what she is about to say.
There is this moon
a new one,
lined up between son and mother,
not invited.

The Escape

Because Mallets Bay is a storm drain
that sucks you in and holds you back
like you're a child who wants to play naked
in the fountains at Roosevelt Field,
while your embarrassed mother pleads for restraint,
because the wind is mutable—
one moment, calm,
a lazy afternoon on the chaise,
the next, the force of a Grand Prix racer
tearing a curve—
Mallets Bay is a prison.

Because Mallets Bay is pear-figured,
fetching, big-hipped, because
her two lips part at the causeway
where she swallows a whole lot of slosh,
we are thwarted with each escape attempt,
sent back to our corner of slips and aluminum docks,
until one day, the wind lets her guard down,
and we slip out.

Volunteering with the Immigrant Mothers

The immigrant mother I work with sits like a good girl,
in front of the computer. To her, the screen is wallpaper,
the monitor, a piece of furniture. Microsoft calls it *Wallpaper*.
She doesn't quite take it in.

The mothers all have smart phones,
but these computers are big and boxy,
they take up space. The donated discards
have no representation in their lives.

How do I convey that a computer is a tool,
like a nail file,
that what they do on one computer,
they can do on another?

This obedient mother has no idea why she is seated in front of a monitor.
Her face is blank.
She clicks, when I say *Click here,*
and hunts the keyboard when I ask her to type.

When I ask her to save her work—
Again, blank. She hunts. Why? What can be saved?
The **Save** icon looks like a floppy disk,
a relic none of these young mothers has ever seen.

My student is oceans away from her original home.
She types her story as one long sentence—
I have two children Jason and Laura
they go Plympton School.

She knows her story by heart.
She doesn't know why she has to tell it to a computer.

Black Trumpets

Because their name is a visual metaphor,
they camouflage the forest floor, because
black is really brown or mauve, because
I take a car and a boat and then walk with my cousin to find them,
because we come from a long line of foragers,
my cousin's mushroom radar is fine-tuned,
because his nimble fingers, because
my sunglasses blur field and foreground,
because the mushrooms smell of apricot, feel like suede,
they have the sweet, deep flavor of earth,
we see the snake we don't know how to name.

Because you can also cook them dried,
they go with well with garlic and eggs.
I would eat them for dessert.
Because there is no currency with higher value,
I feel rich with a full, pungent sack,
although the ones I gather
are mostly shriveled and dark.

Becoming Calm

The forecast was *winds from the east,*
becoming calm in the morning,
which I didn't understand,
until, like that strong north that blew in from nowhere
so hard the dishes clattered from the counter,
you snapped when I offered to shut the motor
halfway through the docking,
but by early the next morning,
ripples settled on the water's surface,
the boats on the moorings, all askew,
you commended my knot-tying,
my unfettered cleats.

The winds are changeable like that,
steady, and then abruptly
a gust, a ninety degree shift,
the whole boat shakes
and the anchor dislodges,
and before you know it
the boat is about to crash into a rock,
like when Diana and I
were on stage for the first time,
Talent Night at the Rec Center,
the ripples of murmurs from the south
began to counter our song,
crescendo to a roar from the west,
and drown our shaky singing
until suddenly,
the tsunami of my cursing
quaked the audience,
and sudden silence,
because at twelve, it was all I knew to do—
to behave as if I could control the elements.

Left Ear

How many sweet nothings have you missed,
tongue gorgings, lost on you,
you, the almost dead one,
the weaker of the two,
who turns away
when someone whispers to you?

But you dangle an earring
as well as your right sister,
who hears incomparably,
so together, the two of you put on a good show,
pretending for me, I am binaural,
like everyone else.

You're my secret weapon in bed—
I nestle my right side into a pillow
and delegate you to face the night's sounds:
the dull rumble of the highway,
the radiator creaking,
the snap of a mouse trap.

At night you are the left ear of anyone's dreams,
until I wake and worry that my right,
tired of carrying the load for two,
might lie down on the job,
steal an early retirement,
or try to meet you halfway.

Imaginary Ice

You know what happens:
You are skiing,
a beautiful, sunny day.
Your partner urges you
to ski on the river.
But the air temperature is just at freezing,
which, for skiing, is warm.

The snow melts,
you say,
from the heat of your skis,
and you see
under his ski-steps,
the mushy gray imprint of slush
and you cringe and whine
about the ice that will surely form
beneath your skis.
I don't want ice,
you say, and he kids you
about imaginary ice.

You predict clumping,
slowing,
as, slipping into the occasional wet,
you continue to glide.
When you stop
and show him
your underneath,
he agrees:
Yes, there is imaginary ice.

Nick Flynn Reads *My Feelings*

In the photo, in yellow and reds,
a laundromat—rather, a Cornell box
of cardboard dryers and washers,
a tiny shirt strewn in checkered red,
miniature carts to move clothes
between the wash and the dry,
presented to us on a big screen
behind Nick
        to distract?
        to enhance?
I am not sure why,
but I find myself hypnotized
by the cycle of Flynn
flailing his arms
to indicate the feelings
he had crossed out on the pages
of his book,
as if no words could ever express those feelings_
while he says, *ineffable*,
uses *ineffable*
more than once or twice
in the book,
a book of poems,
My Feelings,
words he has no word for—
shall I make sense of this
or ask how he does it?
While Flynn performs
his multimedia act,
I picture a video behind the podium,
a representation of me,
performing the ab work I haven't done today—
first, an elephant
lifting his trunk

up and down,
up and down,
then, an airport escalator,
the up, the down,
next the push-pull of pistons
in an engine, my engine,
turned sideways,
and then suddenly a flower,
the whole synchronized team
in a Busby Berkley number,
      in and out
      in and out
and after the elephant trunk,
and the pistons,
topiary clippers
like in the film *Fast, Cheap, and Out of Control*—
The daily workout I miss, my cross outs,
and now I wonder how Flynn does this,
what his special charisma is,
how he says one word,
ineffable
to wild applause.

Holiday

A bicycle ride along a deserted beach.
A finger pointing to the lone yellow parrotfish
in the calm, under the churn.
Cold watermelon, cut into cubes,
shared, under hot sun.
A walk on the beach to photograph the sunset.
Garlic and hot pepper added to the black beans
as they simmer into softness.
A dance with spins and kisses and moonlight.
A seductive smile with *Good morning*.

Gum Surgery

Matter of fact, I was under her knife, a small leaf of upper pallet en route to my gum, when I realized she was telling her assistant an interesting story. I was thinking about raking the leaves, and missed the beginning—the part where she planned to go to the charity ball and meet up with friends, so she found a date to escort her. He seemed so suitable—Picked her up, checked her coat.

I came to, just in time, when the story unfolded that the rake snuck off and left her there. She had lost time from her friends as she leafed through the ballroom for him, needle in a haystack. Finally she texted, and learned from his reply, ever-polite, he had blown her off, she, without a car, in her heels, no money for a cab, in her skimpy dress, leaves of fabric to be blown by the damp harbor winds.

I heard *South Boston. Downtown Crossing. Garden.* I thought about the night characters blowing through the downtown streets like the leaves swirling around her. The thread she pulled through my gum emerged bloody. She threaded it through again.

She thought maybe he didn't like her friends.

I thought, *Date from Hell.*
I thought, *This is my mouth.*
I kept it open.
I said nothing.

Roadside Apples, Vermont

The cars that travel fast
on dirt roads
kick up so much dust,
I shut my eyes
and close my mouth
when they pass.
I gear my bike down
as I climb
the steep hills,
try to avoid
gravel and sand,
so I won't slip.
As I ride,
I don't think
about what I can't do,
rather, what I can,
and each time I pass an apple tree,
I know it from the drops on the road,
and look up to see one
full of ripe,
dust-covered,
neglected apples
that beckon picking.
I think, *Yes, this one,*
I'll come back to later,
these could be my apples—
applesauce,
and make a mental note—
this hill, this road, that barn—
but keep riding,
and think the same thoughts,
make similar mental notes
at the next tree.

Check Engine Light

When the check engine light goes on for the first time in years,
I head out for a bike ride, leave the car safe at home, avoid work.

While I ride, I think. I'd like to think I am a good thinker,
but more often, I empty my head.

But then thoughts sprout like the deep purple mint of early spring,
and I remember the check engine light,

and that there's a paper clip trick to pull the code,
and think *I must remember to Google this.*

I think about my difficulty with remembering what to Google,
and other thoughts come and go, as I pedal as hard as I can.

No matter how fast I pedal, there are super cyclists out there
who pass me on the road.

When after the ride, I sit myself down, I try to quiet my mind,
to not check email, or my bank balance, or search the internet,

but if I am lucky, I might stumble into that distraction
and remember to search about the Check Engine Light, (CEL) I find out,

and as I tumble down a rabbit hole of Honda Repair blogs and video instructions
for pulling the OBII codes without a scanner, just a paper clip,

taking careful notes, I draw a picture of the pinholes to connect,
there is more searching to do, *how to reset the light*, for example,

and before I realize, it's midnight and it's time to quit.
There is always tomorrow, and tomorrow's ride,

after which, I remember the paper clip on top of my car,
and with my headlamp, I find the pins

that yield the code, the secret code, what I am lacking
this time, *Catalyst System.*

Among the Pine Chips

See how it piles up—the pine chip mountain range—
is it better or bitter it should pile so?

From above, the black-winged crows swoop down and rummage.
Is it better, crow, to search for last year's nest in a pile of rubble?

These crows don't care, they pick at piles, they pile needles into questions
until a human wonders from the warmth of her well-lit kitchen,

are you lost, birds? If so, the pines she had felled, did *they* make it so,
when the giants thudded thunder claps to the earth?

But is it home they're after, rooting around the chips?
Are the chips, mounded back there, dive stands for squirrels,

or a reminder of a woman's labors, pitch fork in hand,
the stream of barrows she carts to nourish tree trunks,

fertilize raspberry islands, lilies of the valley, while her efforts
hardly dent the pile? Back at the mound, forkful after forkful,

until the tines stab at something hard, buried deep,
a hobo, still wet with heat, stubbled along its length,

thick as a beansprout ready to take root,
is this bittersweet?

Notes from the Green Room

The pop star tangos on stage
with the mike stand,
his darlin' in hand.

He jumps, but softens the fall,
knees bent, old bones don't cushion
like they used to.

Seventies: The new twenties.
A haggard man, a gentle man,
dressed, and smokin' hot like a steam train.

Hoppin' like a jack rabbit,
Tennessee Williams' poems
gush from his back pocket.

The man who knows the stars,
the bums, the folkies, and the movies,
deals stories like a croupier.

Backstage, shrunken,
delicate as cracked china,
he ices his ankles, neck, knees—

Someone slips off
his slinky satin,
bares the milky flaps of skin.

Houseboat Song

There is a song I sing each morning—
Sun, shine on the roof of solar panels.
Rock us gently in the solar houseboat.

On the shelf, peppercorns and olive oil,
in the cupboard, rice and beans.
There is a song to sing each morning.

In the closet: solar inverter, charge controller,
battery, toaster oven, microwave.
Rock us gently in the solar houseboat.

Sleep right up against the windows.
   The breeze across my face,
   the bullfrog's basso beat,
   the loon mother's lament.
There is a song to sing each morning.

Feel calm sleeping, cooking, trawling, or docked at shore.
When a cloud or darkness obscures the sun, the battery sustains.
Sustain us, rock us gently in the solar houseboat.

A sunset cruise in our *Wake with the Sun,*
the electric motor whirrs, churns a slow boil.
This is the song I sing each evening—
Rock us gently in the solar houseboat.

The Mistake of Cutting Down

I was mistaken I didn't care for the pine trees that bordered my yard—
    The needle-pissers
    The sap-cryers
    The sun-sponges
    The temples of shade

I was mistaken that cutting down trees
would be nothing more than an even exchange
of dollars for work.

I was mistaken my neighbor didn't care when he said so,
mistaken I understood my neighbor understood
what I didn't know I didn't understand.

I was mistaken I would not quiver with each thud and thunder,
mistaken my back yard was not a spring,
rather, a sponge that would not recoil from the trauma of heavy machines.

I accepted a sparse cover
of seed and loam for the future promise of a recovered lawn.
Was that a mistake too?

I was mistaken not to consider the birds,
mistaken I hated squirrels.

I was mistaken a man with ropes on a limb was exciting,
the felling of trees, not violent.

Our Dance

You chassé in from the kitchen,
and I chassé toward you
until we meet,
run in place,
race to catch the first beat of our song,
Sous le Ciel de Paris,
an instrumental version,
rich with harmonica and accordion,
music we know by heart, now,
so as we twist and spin,
braid and unbraid,
your left arm over my right shoulder,
we da-da da-da along,
and settle down
with one last turn,
and kiss
on the final note.

III

Intimacy with the Wind

Speaking of the infinite,
the parade of yachts,
not a parade, the armada
should have been a clue,
while, in golden oblivion,
anchored in the lee at the lip of a bay,
we ate our sandwiches,
until a plate slid off the table
and we looked out the window
at the blackening sky.

The williwaw that rushed in
with the distant storm—
horror on our faces
horror in the water—
thrashed the boat wildly.

Shoes, chairs,
waves swept anything not tied down
off the deck,
and we wondered if we would tip.
The pummeling rain made for shelter
every time we opened the door.

Then, the realization
we were adrift.

The wind that threatened to crash us
into a cliff
almost broke us up
until the moment we engaged the motor
and found out who we were.

Asparagus

A few minutes after hanging up, my father calls back to tell me
three new asparagus are coming up.

I had started the patch from seed at my parents' house, years ago.

Now, my father calls me every time a spear pokes through. With each call,
I am reminded of my shortcomings and feel inept—I'm not sure why.

The soil in that corner of their yard is rich. The crop had barely started to yield
when I moved to a land that forbids overwintering.

I tried, but the transplants failed in Florida.

When I moved back north, I tried to transplant again. This time, the original patch
was so dug in, I could not hack off enough root for the plant to take.

Plus, I had woodchucks and voles.

I still plan to dig up some more asparagus plants,
the next time I visit my father.

And here, the generations are:

Water and soil, and seed, not much bigger than coriander, but smooth as a bearing.
Years and years of waiting, watching, and missing the ones that race to flower and
    reseed.

The key is to catch the plant when it's young,
before it really roots in.

Now, my father gets mature spears. When he finds one just three inches tall,
he gambles on the optimal time to pick. If he waits too long, he says it goes to seed.

What to do with this girl?

I learned to grow raspberries, but not to build fences.
I once battled one groundhog with a shovel, in a world full of groundhogs.

I dreamt my mother helped me dig up some of the plants, and instead of asparagus, she rose from the ground, full, fleshy, green.

Learning to Ride

I.
Those who can
and those who can't—
the able
and the incapable,
a separable set,
but every day
someone on this earth
makes the leap,
balance and momentum,
learns to ride,
how to lean
into a turn
and not ground.

II.
There was a girl whose father
told her it was time to remove the extra wheels.
She was afraid she would fall off,
but her father ran with the girl
and her blue bike,
as he told her how he never rode a bike as a boy,
growing up poor in the city,
he had no need to learn,
his parents couldn't even afford his new shoes,
so when he was 22, in graduate school,
he taught himself to ride
on a country road
the day he understood
rolling resistance,
that two wheels attached to a frame
are inherently stable when set in motion,
and she kept on pedaling
when he let her go.

III.
Most people learn to ride as children,
but some never learn,
like the woman who grew up in Mumbai.
She sees her young son master his,
and stares, forlorn,
into the space
once occupied
by her son, his bike.

To a Spur Trail

You peek out from behind a knocked down old fence,
a sliver of silk scarf, orange flutter in the wind.

Entreat me, your Gretel, with your dazzling jewels.
Dappled sunlight at your feet,

a moth lingers between your sedges, flits and hops.
You hug tight a tree stump, felled for your making,

a severed umbilical, an outie,
protruding like a young boy's belly.

You draw my eye there, so I don't stumble.
Unwitting leader, you model tree limbs on your runway,

twirl in the wind, and point me toward the old stone boundary,
the thick of green all around.

Wearer of earth scents, of pine needles,
dead wood, and brush.

Sculpture in the museum of natural beauty,
you teach me to find my way

along your thick parts and narrow,
your hard pack and the runoff-moistened mud.

Teaser, siren, you lead me
to what must have been a stream in spring,

now, muddy and soft. What is it about this stream
that begs crossing? What holds me back?

Is it simply the water, where I can sit and listen,
read closely the darkness that separates one leg

from the other, or, am I driven to follow you,
no matter the muck you lure me through?

Gummi

Today I'm thinking of those Chinese jump ropes, our gummi ropes,
elastic loops wrapped in gray nylon with silver threads woven through—

smooth and sparkly when new, and later, scratchy with age. My mom bought them
at FAO Schwarz, one for my sister, one for me, back when my sister and I

shared a bedroom, where she coaxed me to practice falling backward
from standing on my mattress, until once, I hit my head on the frame.

Gummi requires three people, or you could substitute a chair
for a person. Two girls stretch the rope in moderate tension

around their ankles, while the jumper crosses the loop
and jumps, catches the rope with her ankle, or lands on it,

performing simple and intricate designs until she falls out,
while the posted girls raise the rope height, if she doesn't.

Did I learn *modulus of elasticity* from that jump rope or from my sister
when I demanded she *Give it back, Give it back, Please, give it back,*

me, holding the gummi rope at one end of the bedroom, she, at the other,
stretching the rope to its limit, until finally, she relented,

and the rope snapped, like a slingshot, into my eye?
Oh, I learned. My cornea is long-healed,

and our parents banned the ropes after that. Why do I remember this now,
when I talk with my sister on the phone, each of us, with silver-stranded hair?

When did she take on such strain? She imagines scenarios
for our aging father: *He will be in diapers, and the caregivers will rob us blind.*

How do I understand *Are you walking around with your head in the sand?*
as an endearment?

Invasive Species

1.
A small fountain of buckthorn
blooms from the base of the maple.

The ribbed leaves,
freshly green, shiny, alluring.

The freckled maroon stems
look so harmless.

2.
Clusters of multiflora rose
emerge there, too.

A bouquet of serrated leaves,
mock sweetness.

Tug the root
when the plant is small.

3.
And tug and tug the bittersweet,
its birch-like leaves, innocent,

but oh, the root, the orange root,
oh, the sorrow.

4.
The buried poison ivy vine,
has reddish leaves in early spring.

Shiny or matted, avoid touch.
Pick, and be punished.

5.
The persistent honeysuckle,
its money leaves, its trumpet flowers,

yields sweet nectar when you pull a stamen.
Roots, too knotted, to remove.

6.
Trim the fire bushes, before they bloom,
before they flame.

7.
The white lace of sweet garlic mustard, pick it!
Pick before the seeds, like dust, scatter.

Cormorant Convention

We smell the fish
before we see the cormorants,
loons and seagulls, too—
and now they gather
at their supermarket,
where Otter Creek
meets the lake.

They dart and dive,
surf a wave
at the river mouth,
where mouths open
and fill.

Snapshots

This is me in July, opening the garden gate,
camera in hand, smiling
at the welcome surprise of summer's first beans,

feeling lucky that *local* is just a matter of feet. This is me
on my bike, right after my father removed the training wheels,
gripping the handlebars.

Something like uncertainty crosses my face,
as he holds onto the back of my seat and runs alongside. This one, me,
soaking in the deep-rose-solstice-sunset horizon clouds,

wondering what the other picnickers feast on,
their faces reflecting the pink when our gazes lock,
while I pick at rotisserie chicken and salad.

This is me nurturing the pot plant I named
for the boy I loved who fled, while the plant thrives
next to my bed. This is me in the throes of a fever

that steals my sleep, my mother wiping my forehead
as she notices the plant next to the bed. Here, even younger,
this is me, running to beat the alligators

waiting to attack me as I leap across the room
and into bed after turning out the lights.
In a baby picture,

I hold an inflatable alligator,
we smile at each other.
This is me now, bleeding,

when I knock my shin hard, into the skeg
of my board, the blood clotted there,
a pointillistic rose.

September, Champlain

Not all marinas are alike,
but most don't call back if you leave a message.

Up and down the coast, people told how great Shelburne is—
real people, plainspoken, like buttered toast.

But these buttered toast people
didn't know us from a stone on the driveway,

Because we are few miles south,
but the caller ID says Massachusetts,

they tell us to call after five,
but they close at five,

and that's how we learn you have to show up—
here you have to show up to do business.

Because the North Hero Marina consists of a tiki bar and an outhouse,
easily reached by bike, but not by boat, we move on.

Because the summer must infallibly end,
we set our sights on September,

and with cooked lentils in the fridge,
an island is as good a destination as a tray of oysters, a smoothie on the deck.

Because

>   Oliver Sachs
>   aging
>   dreams
>   ferns
>   apples
>   blue-green algae
>   cow manure—

Because we still haven't lined up a marina to pull us out,
we call another—the well, too narrow, the lift, not rated for our weight.

Because another causeway, an inland sea. Because
landowners on Butler Island share a walking path,

because solar or nothing, and savory food cooked on a fire,
we find new friends by just showing up.

Because one guy with a travel lift and a wide-enough well
showers once a week and responds to a compliment, he says *Yes*,

money says, *Yes*. Because the man lives on his boat
until he can close up shop and head to Florida,

he spits when he sees *Bernie* plastered to the back of a pickup.
Because the green algae soup drives us away,

a rock cliff juts up from the deep clear,
a stream settles in a bed of sand.

Shadows through the Window

A ladybug, crawling on the window,
walks across my page.

A bird in flight
flits along the strips of my sheets.

Now, the wind,
a flutter of yellow leaves stipples the wall.

Clouds draw a gray shadow
& for a moment, still.

Look up, motion.
Soon, once more, sun.

Hot and Cold

You take the rolls from the freezer and toss them into the toaster oven.
The smoothie is this: yogurt, almonds, frozen blueberries.
Your rolls take 5 minutes, mine, 40 seconds.
Add chia seeds and a frozen banana, if you have one.
They soften with heat.
Fill in the interstitials with almond milk.
I press **Add 30** on the microwave and wait.
Blend together.

After the ding, I remove the bowl, turn over the roll and feel.
The blue cream is thick and stiff.
I place the roll back in for another 10 or 12 seconds.
Split it out to share.
Baked in the toaster oven, the rolls are hot and soft. Mine harden fast.
Before placing the spoon in your mouth, prepare for cold.
I bounce one between my hands to cool it
until I can tear the flesh and insert some cheese.
Brain freeze.
Once in the mouth, feel the heat.
Blow on it this way, huhhh, to warm it up.
Blow to cool, and chew your roll.
Wonder why, on this cold, gray day, a smoothie.

Everywhere, the Light

The light comes in from everywhere
Nothing curtains wouldn't mute
Shades escaped your intricate plans
for a house of light, the tiny house of light.

Nothing curtains couldn't mute,
except the joyous sounds we make.
In the house of light, the tiny house of light,
we shed our clothes and agitate.

Except for our joyous trumpeting
as we rock the bed with the streaming sun.
We shed our clothes and agitate
the worms in the garden, the squirrels in the trees.

As we rock the bed with the streaming sun,
I turn and catch, from the corner of my eye
next to the wormy garden, beneath the squirrely trees,
your mother, knocking at the door.

I turn to catch, out the corner of my eye,
through the naked shades that escaped your intricate plan,
from behind your mother, knocking at the door,
light pours in from everywhere.

Oh, Thistle

Oh, Thistle,
you need so little in life,
how did you make your way here?
Who were you trying to please?
Did you aim to marry the iris,
or to die under the yew?

Too, Thistle,
you need so little in life,
what do you want to say?
(let's get to the point, eh?)
You slipped in so quietly, I didn't notice,
and here you are, slipped in again.

You, Thistle,
you need so little in life,
don't you want to die?
Your roots are so shallow.
You've made so many mistakes.
You want to live without loving.

Too, Thistle,
you give so little in life,
would you ever sense its poetry?
Your life, entire, done, is nothing.
Your tiny feelings, effected
by your unmade house.

Late for Dinner

It's 7:35 PM in Truro and I count out the miles as I turn off route 6.
I follow the pocked dirt road I know as well as my back yard
to check in with my cousin, unannounced, except for the sheep
bleating and the horses and the clucky chickens.

I think, *one minute*. I'll just stay one minute.
Say *Hi*. Say *Bye*.
So I leave the car parked crooked
protruding a little into the driveway.

When I see Mike step onto the deck
to find out why the little dachshunds are yapping,
I wave, but he's already heading inside,
saying, *Come on up*.

After the stairs and the hugs,
he shows me the solar panels
he just bought online for his houseboat
and mentions a propane toilet, stove, and heater.

I think fire. Imagine burning.
Why not all solar, all electric?
Why don't I remember
watts are energy per unit time?

I was supposed to be elsewhere by then, dinner, at 8.
As cousin time clicks out web pages—
blood thicker than wine—
I'm late to the dinner table.

My lover and friends, all very nice,
already eating the deliciously orchestrated meal
whose flavors I try to pick out. I make apologies for lateness,
mistaking balsamic vinegar for *interesting*.

Bedrooms

Your room
was yours
because
I got there
first
the new house
had a third
floor but
my room
was mine
because
of the sun.

In my room
two windows
south
and one east
and a higher
ceiling
than yours
Mom built
shelves
across the two
for plants
the sun
would feed
I would water
She didn't know
about the pot
plant until
I had mono
a kiss
on my forehead
and a sharp eye
I loved my room
the sun
the heat

until
when you left
home I slipped
upstairs
a fugitive
from our parents
to the lone single bed
my head
to the south
wall
in your room
of weak sun
with only
two east-facing
windows
One rule
I was not permitted
heat
so I sought
warmth
other ways
the late night
synchronized creak
a young man's feet
behind mine.

Mom used
my old room
as her office
after I left home
She spent
her last days
there
in an
adjustable bed
until once
she lifted herself
gleaming
to the sun.

Dream

In the dream
I don't quite remember,
a man, uneducated,
or uncultured,
or both,
he was some kind of thug,
or taxi driver
who met me once or twice—
like the elevator operator
I met in Cuba,
the one who used Chinese condoms
that only half-fit,
as if to signify that Chinese equipment
is on the small side,
or maybe these are the only ones
the Chinese government was willing to donate to Cubans
because they cost less,
more bang for the buck—
fell for me, I am not sure how,
as I doubt I said much of anything in this dream,
but the man, in his thugness
was a perfect gentleman—
a walk along the river
and ambling drive in his cab
and somehow, that's just the way dreams work,
I knew he was poised to propose marriage,
so I fell into that state of confusion,
that inability to act,
to own up to my feelings
and counter the flattery,
but when he sent a woman to see me,
presumably a marriage broker
who would gently convey the man's intention,
My honey pie,
my true love appeared,
and I told him I loved him
in front of the woman,

and held his hand in mine
like we were glued together,
so that when the man drove up in his cab,
or walked up to us with his thug buddies and balloons—
far more romantic than the elevator operator with his emails—
my lover and I kissed and kissed
until even an uncultured criminal
would understand
love cannot be invented
or dreamt up
or bought.

IV

Invasive Species on the Trail

Glossy buckthorn,
multiflora,
they're all over.
The bees are entranced
by the nose
but this is not your garden,
multiflora rose,
nor yours honeysuckle,
sweet garlic mustard,
Japanese knotweed.

Who do you think you are,
to command such presence,
like some bejeweled dress of wire
hanging from a tree?
Has no one told you,
you don't belong here?
Yes, we are all wanderers
but your heart,
your heart is in the wrong place.

Valcour

If it weren't for the marina,
and the crane, one of whose stabilizing legs,
with its hydraulic shaft
dangling loose, twisted like a broken limb,
and the cracked windshield, half-gone,
but whose operator,
(half-empty rum bottle on the porch table),
expert enough to know where to hang his chains
across the spreader bar
to lift 5000 pounds of house
onto the pontoon boat,
but not before the hard work of the long drive
to put the boat together,
then the wind and rain that first day,
the calm motoring next days,
the small bays,
the curious questions
about the "floating house,"
from other boaters
(build it yourselves?)
all solar, all electric,
and if not for those solar panels,
the battery, the electric motor,
dancing on the deck,
the need for provisions,
the folding bikes piled into the kayak
and the country bike ride
to fetch groceries,
the delectable meals,
eggs, solar-side up,
the waylay in Burlington,
its restaurants
the bike path,
solar popcorn,
meals with friends,
following winds,
thwarting winds,

winds that threatened to wreck the boat—
if it weren't for the knocking waves,
the crashing waves
that splashed up through the deck,
and our added caution,
and finally, one calm sunny day,
our crossing the big open lake,
the anchor set for safe harbor in a cove,
smoothies on the back porch,
our back 40
inches of decking,
all this, and the sun
that freed us
from roads,
marinas,
traffic,
if not for a spoonful of the ice-cold,
the pure,
the creamy,
this would not be
our Valcour,
our victory.

My Orchard

What's left of the large pines
I had cut down last winter
is dead now.

Garlic mustard,
Virginia creeper,
poison ivy
thrive in their place.

My neighbor asks, "What are your plans for the area?"
First thought, *no plan.*

The ground, uneven, littered with remnants,
weed trees I sawed down in past seasons.
New growth sprouts from Norway maple and buckthorn stumps.

Where she sees mess,
I see canvas.

I planted three peach pits today.
Three apricot seeds, and a whole cherry.
I transplanted blueberry plants
dug from the woods.

Thistle, bittersweet,
prick and strangle.

And the jewelweed—
Oh, "nuisance."
Oh, orchard.

Sunshine State

The sun warms my face, as I nap on the couch,
long and firm, comfortable, and settled
in the sunroom for all these years.

It is a napping couch,
a kissing and cajoling couch.

Once, when I moved apartments,
Two students hefted the couch,
too long to fit the elevator,
so they spiraled it lengthwise,
up five flights, while you directed.

Moving companies handled all of my other moves.
The couch, with its wobble and decrepit foam,
came along each time, even though you scolded me for it—
Too ugly.
Too heavy.
Monstrosity, (your favorite word).

Thanks to a friend, I found a woman
to replace the foam and reupholster the couch
in floral fabric—each hydrangea, aligned and centered.

Something to make you happy, Mother.

That time, you didn't complain
when I told you I would move it north, from Florida,
I didn't have a digital camera,
so you took my word for it.

Ever since, I have told and retold the story of the couch
you hated, and later embraced,
its fabric, still proudly efficient, but faded,
like me napping here
on this couch
in the sunshine.

Before We Know Darkness

Before *WalkMen*. Before *iPods*. Before we know better,
we hop on a subway uptown, two young teens.

This is 1974, the year of the Laserium, the laser show that
lights the night sky of the Hayden Planetarium.

Dark Side of the Moon marries the haze of the good reefer
Julie and I roll expertly between the two fingers of each hand,

careful not to tear the paper as we lick the gum band and twist the ends.
The swish-flare of match, and with a deep hiss-suck, it lights.

We smoke to the change-clink of *Money*.
We hop the Express by mistake.

Waiting for the Local to sweep us back from Harlem,
a man, tall as the train and dark as the ties, shoots, *Got five dollars to spare?*

If I push you over the tracks, would you have five dollars?
J. flips, *Pushing us won't make five dollars appear.*

I am scared. He needs his smack.
We suck in the relief as he turns away.

Suffering time before the train arrives,
cradled in jugga-jugga-jugga, we think we are safe.

In the near-empty car, out from behind a gray trench coat,
a flash of whole prick.

We are teens with stories in our pockets.
We move to the next car before anyone smells our fear.

A Passion Fruit

I bought a durian for you, that frozen wooden spiked football of a fruit,
my devotion to your passion for exotic foods.
I roamed the Sydney market streets alone, thinking of you back in Vermont.

Barely forewarned, this was not a thing likely pleasant,
I persisted—I heard Malaysians loved durian
and I loved you.

You would not forgive me if I passed up the durian once more,
so I bought the frozen bastard—all ten dollars of it,
and waited until it thawed, while more people told me how much it smelled.

I laughed to myself a lot about this passion, until the time for the cutting.
I was breaking a fast from food poisoning,
when hotel chef brought me the creamy, mushy pulp—

It tasted of raw onions,
smelled of rotten eggs.

To Abuse

Abuse, holed up in a corner, you're sneaky.
You wear gym shorts under sweats,
go unnoticed, fit in, totally.

Last time, I almost missed you,
but then your snake tongue lashed out—
shouts and a shove in the name of, what, love?

It's only later, alone, I recognize you. I lag in that way.
From a distance, you don't seem so scary,
and I relax.

But next time, next time, Abuse, I'll be ready.
I will tear into your sweats,
expose your hot pink shorts.

Something from Nothing

The morning we have to leave the inn,
food, beginning to thin,
no eggs, but a few frozen slices of bread,
cheese, two chicken sausages,
and one well-traveled Butler island tomato,
picked green the week before, now, red,
so, while toasting the bread,
I slice the sausages into rings,
cut the tomato into three sandwich slices
and two ends,
and on two of the toast slices,
sprinkle hot chili oil,
then garlic powder,
then za'atar,
and to this, I add tomato,
one slice per toast,
and a third slice, quartered,
to fit around the corners,
then the sausage rings,
topped with cheddar,
plus some za'atar on the two tomato ends
placed next to the two toasts,
and into the microwave,
2:22 (easy on the fingers),
and finally, top the open sandwiches
with the remaining toast,
and serve warm,
like love,
something out of nothing.

In My Yard

1. The Raspberries

The raspberries know that it takes confidence to get by in the world.
But what does a construction worker, for example, know about anger management?
Up on her ladder, her hammer wails on the deck stairs, forcing them into place.
Maybe she knows quite a bit.

We might take comfort, after work,
seated at the kitchen table,
rubbing a cup of raspberry tea,
raising it to our lips,
looking out at our raspberry patch,
the foliage, light green.

2. Rabbits

Rabbits are not just gray,
but combine gray with brown, hazel, & pure white.
Even some black
threads through the fur.

This one sits and wriggles its nose
until spooked.

I have difficulty describing the rabbit in my yard
without thinking of trapping it
in my Havahart.

3. The Glossy Buckthorn near the Maple

Glossy buckthorn, you remind me
of photographic paper, male deer,
Our Town, invasive plant species,
chest wall strains, stubbornness,
trout skeleta, and the bittersweet
you're so chummy with,
(in that order).

4. Sweet Garlic Mustard

There are so many of them,
fat, squat, bouquets,
and once bloomed, skinny skewers,
flowers so white, nothing could be purer.
Sometimes you forget they seed like
the rabbits breed, & spread & root,
not just one tap root, a network of capillaries.

Then you think how lucky it is you have all this
painful mustard growing in your side yard,
when you trouble to photograph it.

5. Virginia Creeper

Virginia, such a sweet, unassuming name,
your pinwheel leaves, your tendrils, so dainty.

But clearly, your ancestry, the *Creeper* clan,
wielded its devil power and was labeled for it.

Virginia creeper, you must have a hard time at the shrink,
claiming you saw God as a child, and what harm could you do?

Your vines, some thin, others thicker than twigs,
grow low, hidden, and inch across my garden.

Suddenly, a new leaf.

I tug your root.
Tug. Tug.

Sometimes you yield,
sometimes, you dig in.

On the Ocean

big enough to hold many griefs—
downed planes, unseaworthy boats,
on the ocean, on a rented boat,
we took turns
to sprinkle the ashes.

The sea burial wasn't easy.
We had not arranged for the wind
that pushed back,
you, covered in mother and brother,
while the roses drifted in pairs,
a fleck of bone on the side of the boat.

Afterward you took to your bed,
having inhaled too many
lives.

Solar House Living

        Sunlight to current
to evening light.
         Streams of people
ripples of questions,
             waves of ideas.
Eddies of conversation
       swirl around the windowed room,
one room that is many—
       kitchen, dining, living, sleeping—
and swoop along the curved ceiling,
         the wooden walls,
            with light.

Light, energy
    energy, power
       ideas, talk, dreams,
     clouds of them,
          and laughter

direct
   alternating,
       the sun, the ebb and flow of energy
    battery, sun, battery.

One small ecosystem.

   With each day,
  with each new visitor,
more wonder,   more questions.

The Sad Ballad of the Garlic Mustard

As a teen, I never thought of Carson as a woman,
maybe it was that hard, masculine name,
but I must have identified more with Miss Amelia,
and her hard ways, turned soft by love,
than with Cousin Lymon.

I felt uncomfortable about Lymon.
He popped up like the garlic mustard
that emerged in my side yard this April.
Not entirely unwelcome,
the punchy green heart-shaped leaves,
bouquets, brides might throw
to hopeful singles. I never caught a bouquet,
but I hoped.

The roots are tender, white, and radishy.
I intended to jettison them,
but then read you can cook them.
I would have to soak the roots
to remove the mud. Miss Amelia
might have used the leaves in a beer.
She would bring out pitchers
and pour glasses all around
while Lymon stayed on.

I could open a popup café with all this mustard:
> Sautéed in eggs,
> a mustard pesto,
> roots, cooked into sauce.

Then, I read the young ones have more cyanide
than the second-years do.
Bad things can go good.
I stare out at all the mustard,
bagsful in my future,
and wonder if I can tackle all this alone,
if I might one day come to love my yard,
if sautéing an invasive is sweet revenge.

Raspberry Season

As I was picking the raspberries
in my yard, where the berries
ripen daily into October,

the bees, dancing in and out,
of the branches, & my fingers,
while picking raspberries,

I noticed a multiflora rose,
baring her menacing hips, her seeds,
and grabbed my clippers, before I would forget.

Soon, the raspberry leaves will shrivel,
leave only thorns and unripened fruit
surprised in the morning by a killing frost.

Until then, I make the rounds,
make them twice, to find one crown
hidden under brittle leaves.

Rose and raspberry thorns
scratch my arms as I reach
for the sweet fruit,

like some omniscient protector
saving the berries for more deserving fingers,
or a rabbit, or slug, or bird.

I pick the raspberries
behind my house,
where the berries bear into October,

and the dwindling
portends winter.

My Netherland

I had planned
a brief, stealth planting,
in-and-out,
a bee in the flower's mouth.

My hair, wet
under cap,
henna drooling down my cheek,
hoping not to meet anyone.

My neighbor walks over,
asks again
about my plans for my yard,
the undergrowth,
where the trees came down.

Mint, raspberries, fruit trees—
The garden of my dreams
streams from my mouth
over the wild mustard,
poison ivy, and bittersweet
that almost have me beat.

I say *thank you*.
She answers, *regulations*,
wild animals.

Later, after the digging, the yanking,
the spray of soil in my hair,
in the shower,
I feel an itch, mid-back,
where I cannot reach.

In the mirror,
a very small neighbor,
merged inseparably
with my skin,
a tick,
a mustard seed
of a tick.

Reasons, November

For Will

If Summer, then motorcycle,
four-stroke, bare-headed.

Then sun, then blare, then burn.
Tiene sueños, uno sombrero.

If Summer, then tomorrow wears shades,
naranjas, smiling in a bowl.

Then Panama. Then eyes open.
Then hope.

If August, then a Route 66 family selfie,
all three, squinting, grinning.

If August, then thin and prune,
then uproot the overspreading lilies.

If September, then college senior—
       hang out on the stoop,
       half-empty bottle,
       acoustic guitar.

If October, then floods,
longed-for rain soaks the parched.

If October, then Halloween,
a lanky young man, dressed as a bear.

If Halloween,
then needle.

Then vein.
If needle, why, needle?

If kidneys, if only.
If November, then turn back time.

Crisis, 1962

Our father might have said,
You're nuts.
Kennedy can handle this.
Don't go.

All over the television
talking heads, talking their heads off.
We were too young to understand—
our nervous mother's, *Where can we go?*
We have to get out of here.

Jugs of water and batteries
vanished from grocery stores—
New York, a sure target.
Then, lunch-packing—
peanut butter and apple butter.

Did their friend, Jim, another refugee,
infect our mother,
or, was it the Kristallnacht shards
imprinted on her little girl eyes
that fed Jim's frenzy?

What tipped their scales?
When, during the 13 days, did they flee?
Whatever, it must have been a bad translation.
Upstate New York, their haven
for the potentially bombed.

Maybe a door slammed,
a motor revved.
Packed into the car,
we girls, voiceless,
left our father with the fallout.

Rings

Saw down a tree and the rings of cellulose
tell the age. I'm not as old as these trees,
and my ring finger is small,
but swells with heat. I wear rings
infrequently. I used to wear an onyx
for good luck. Where is that ring now?
The only wedding band I have
is the one my mother gave to me
just before she died,
hoping I might have use for the ring,
flourished with a wing of diamonds.
I wear it when I want to feel wedded,
as I wake in my double bed,
stare out at the emptiness
where my trees once stood,
and listen to the caw of crows,
the coo of mourning doves
who mate for life,
a lone one there, perched on a wire,
a pink band of sunlight around her neck.

Acknowledgements

A sincere thank you to Fred Marchant for reading the manuscript prior to publication, and for his wisdom and generosity as a poet, teacher, and friend. The author would also like to thank Alan Feldman, Bernard Horn, and the participants of the Tuesday night library poetry workshop for their suggestions and inspiration for the early drafts of some poems in this manuscript. Thank you also to my family and friends, for your encouragement and love. Also a big thank you to all who have preordered this book, to help determine the press run. Finally, thank you to Claude von Roesgen, for your love, encouragement, and living the dream.

The author is also grateful to the editors of the following publications for publishing previous versions of some of the poems in this collection.

"Asparagus," *The Mom Egg*, Spring, 2017.
"At Breakfast," *The Wild Word*, 2016.
"Aubade Champlain," *ArLiJo* #90, 2016.
"Becoming Calm," *ArLiJo* #90, 2016.
"Before We Know Darkness," Juvenessence issue of *The Fourth River Review*, 2017.
"Black Trumpets," *Switched-On Gutenberg*, 2015.
"City Bay to Butler Island in the Solar-powered Boat," *The Provo Canyon Review*, 2016.
"Comment se Faire," *Sunday Poet*, Boston Area Small Press and Poetry Scene Blog, 03/27/16.
"Crisis, 1962," Juvenessence issue of *The Fourth River Review*, 2017.
"Gum Surgery," *City of Notions: An Anthology of Contemporary Boston Poems*, 2017.
"Dream," *Poetry Quarterly*, 2016, and reprinted at *Soul-Lit*, volume 17, Summer, 2017.
"Everywhere the Light," *Ibbetson Street Magazine*, Volume 35, 2015.
"Holiday," *First Literary Review-East*, 2016.
"Hot and Cold," *Eyedrum, Fusion Issue*, 2016.
"Imaginary Ice," *Tell-Tale Inklings* #2, 2016.
"Invasive Species, Part 6." *Plum Tree Tavern*, 2016.
"Late for Dinner," semi-finalist, 2014 *Naugatuck River Review* narrative poetry contest, 2015.
"Lost Hour," *Inkstain Press*, 2016.

"My Father's Hiking Boots," *Wayne Review*, 2017, and reprinted at *Soul-Lit*, volume 17, Summer, 2017.
"My Netherland," *The Lake*, 2017.
"My Orchard," *Aurorean*, 2016.
"Nick Flynn Reads My Feelings," *SHARKPACK Poetry Review*, 2017.
"Oh Thistle," *Alchemy*, 2017.
"Our Dance," *First Literary Review-East*, 2016.
"Passion Fruit," *Gyroscope Review*, 2017.
"Photoshopping the Body," *Sweet Tree Review*, July, 2017.
"Solar House Living," *Pinyon Review*, 2017.
"Sunshine State," *Tell-Tale Inklings* #2, 2016.
"To a Spur Trail," *Poetry on the Trail, Hopkinton Center for the Arts,* 2015.
"To Seize the Ice," *Ibbetson Street Magazine*, Fall/Winter 2016/2017.
"Trying to Leave Mallets Bay," *Panoply Zine*, Spring/Summer 2016.

Carla Schwartz is a poet, blogger, filmmaker, photographer, and lyricist. Her first book of poems, *Mother, One More Thing* is available through Turning Point Books (2014). Her poem, *In Defense of Peaches*, was a Massachusetts Poetry Foundation Poem of the Moment. Her poem, *Late for Dinner,* was a semifinalist for the Naugatuck River Review Narrative Poetry Contest. She organized the session, *Poetry of the Body* for the 2014 Massachusetts Poetry Festival. Her poem, *Gum Surgery,* was selected for the Mayor of Boston 2017 Poetry Program for public poetry at Boston City Hall. She makes poetry, documentary, and instructional videos. Her CB99videos youtube videos have had 1,600,000+ views. She has performed her work in the U.S., Canada, and Australia. Carla is also a professional writer with a doctoral degree from Princeton University. She has more than 800 Facebook friends and 2600 youtube subscribers. Learn more at her website at carlapoet.com. Check her blog at wakewiththesun.blogspot.com. Follow her @cb99videos.

www.ingramcontent.com/pod-product-compliance
Lightning Source LLC
Chambersburg PA
CBHW070549090426
42735CB00013B/3118